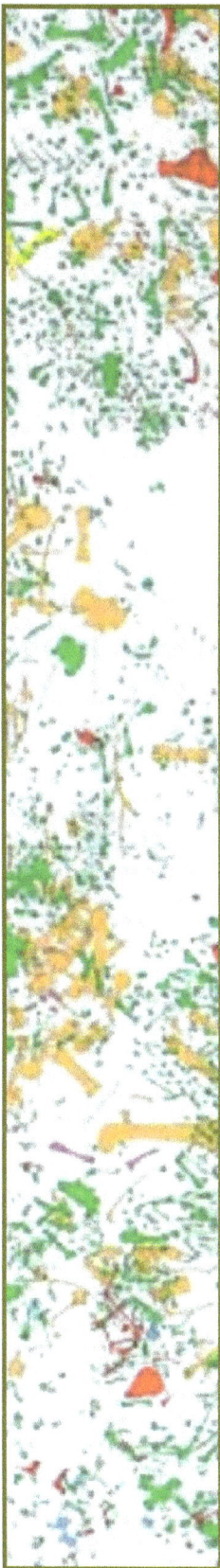

What is a Jurassic Explorer?

As a Jurassic Explorer, it is your responsibility to preserve and protect your public lands, care for your natural and cultural resources, and to share what you have learned with others. Protecting our public lands preserves them for the enjoyment of present and future generations.

This book contains information and activities about Cleveland-Lloyd Dinosaur Quarry. It is designed to help you discover and investigate the mystery of Cleveland-Lloyd. This site has been known about for over 80 years and we still don't have a good explanation as to what happened here.

Complete the activities alone or with the help of a friend or parent. When you're done, show your case file to the visitor center staff and you will earn the status of Jurassic Explorer.

I0189940

What is the Bureau of Land Management (BLM)?

The Bureau of Land Management was formed in 1946 by combining the Grazing Service and the General Land Office.

The BLM is responsible for carrying out a variety of programs for the management and conservation of resources on 245 million surface acres, as well as 700 million acres of subsurface mineral estate. The Bureau manages more public land than any other federal agency.

Cleveland-Lloyd Dinosaur Quarry has the first visitors' center managed by the BLM. The visitor's center was dedicated in 1968 and renovated in 2006. The Cleveland-Lloyd Dinosaur Quarry was declared a National Natural Landmark in 1966.

North quarry building

To get started, ask a staff member to tell you the story of Cleveland-Lloyd. When you're done, you'll get a stamp to place in the box.

Welcome to Cleveland-Lloyd Dinosaur Quarry

Look at the display in the visitors' center to answer the following questions about the history of Cleveland-Lloyd.

1. University of Utah _____ investigated the area in 1928 and 1929 and unearthed about 500 bones.

2. _____ grew up in the nearby town of Cleveland.

3. _____,a lawyer in Philadelphia, donated $10,000 to fund the excavation of the quarry in 1941.

4. What kinds of details are studied in the deposit?

5. In _____, the University of Utah began excavation in cooperation with several universities and museums.

6. Much of the work was done by _____ under the direction of _____.

7. Paleontologists now understand that _____ alone don't tell the whole story.

How do you measure up?

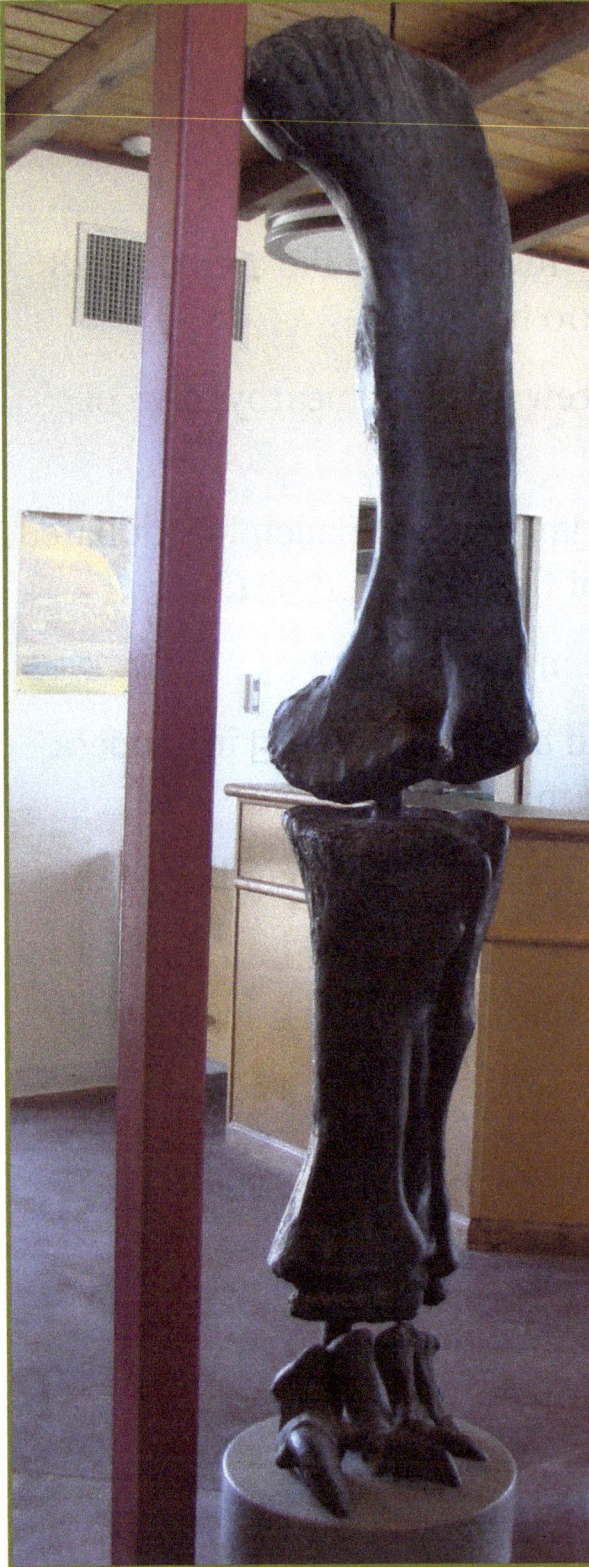

Take a look at the cast of the Camarasaur leg in the visitor's center. The *Camarasaurus* is a type of dinosaur known as a sauropod. They ate plants and so they are called herbivores. They would have no trouble peeking into your second-floor window.

Stand next to the leg and see how you measure up. Mark your height on the picture of the leg on this page.

Where did all the bones go?

The bones from Cleveland-Lloyd have been sent to museums all over the US and the world. Look at the world map in the visitors' center to answer the questions below.

1. Where are you from? Are there any bones from Cleveland-Lloyd in your home state?

   _____

2. List 3 countries other than the United States that have bones from Cleveland-Lloyd Dinosaur Quarry.

   _____

3. Look at the museums listed on the panel. From the list of museums, name a museum other than Cleveland-Lloyd that you have visited or would like to visit.

   _____

What Should You Bring?

There are many great places to go hiking around Cleveland-Lloyd. The trails can be fun, but they can also be dangerous if you're not prepared.

Look at the pictures below and circle the items that you should bring. Cross out the ones you should leave at home.

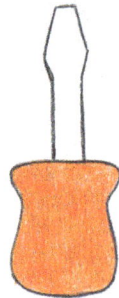

Fossilization

The word paleontology means the study of ancient life. A paleontologist is someone who studies ancient life. Paleontologists try to piece together what an animal from long ago looked like, where they lived, and what they ate. They have to rely on fossils as their evidence.

A fossil is the preserved remains or traces of an animal from the distant past. There are many different kinds of fossils. Fossilization will only take place under very special circumstances. Not every animal becomes a fossil.

An animal dies and over time its bones are buried.

Some remains can be petrified. This means that the remains were literally turned to stone. Microscopic spaces in the bones, teeth, or shells become filled with minerals. The bones at Cleveland-Lloyd have been petrified.

Some fossils are called trace fossils because they give evidence that something alive had been there but no part of the animal is found.

Look around the visitors' center and you will find examples of both kinds of fossils.

Carnivores and Herbivores

There are two types of dinosaurs. The dinosaurs that eat plants are called herbivores and those that eat meat are called carnivores.

Complete the maze and help the allosaur find his meal.

Jurassic Explorer Safety Scrambler

Unscramble the sentences below to learn how to explore safely.
Write the unscrambled sentences on the line.

1. alone. hike Never

_____

2. of water. plenty Be sure to bring

_____

3. marked Always trails. stay on the

_____

4. animals. Don't touch wild.

_____

Dinosaurs at **CLDQ**

Look at the display in the visitors' center for clues about each dinosaur. Draw a line from the dinosaur to its description.

Allosaurus

This carnivore is known for its small horns above the eyes and large horn on its nose. It is unlikely that the large horn was used for a weapon.

Stegosaurus

A powerfully built flesh eater with huge teeth and savage claws. This is one of the biggest late Jurassic carnivores.

Camarasaurus

One of the few plated dinosaurs that were found in western North America. This dinosaur was an herbivore with large triangular plates arranged along its back.

Ceratosaurus

This long necked plant eater is one of the best studied of the sauropods. It was the first sauropod to be discovered with its skull.

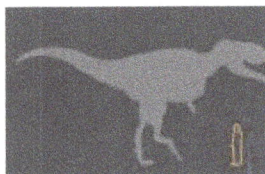

Torvosaurus

There were 46 of these found at Cleveland–Lloyd. These animals were carnivores. A distinguishing characteristic is the presence of a small bony crest just above and forward of each eye.

What is a Cultural or Natural Resource?

Places like Cleveland–Lloyd exist to protect cultural and natural resources so they will be here for everyone to enjoy and learn about.

A **cultural resource** is something that tells the story of the people that came before us.

A **natural resource** can be plants, animals, water, or scenery. It is anything that is not made by humans.

Look at the pictures below and read the description. Circle C if it is a cultural resource, or circle N if it is a natural resource.

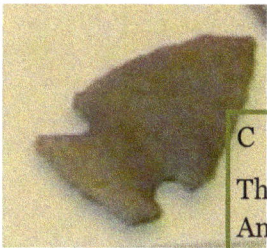

C N

This arrowhead was made by American Indians 1,000 to 1,500 years ago. They used flint from local sources as well as trading for it with other Indians.

C N

This is a Pilling Figurine, named after Clarence Pilling, who discovered them in a cave in a side canyon of Range Creek back in 1950. They are approximately 800-900 years old.

C N

This is an allosaur's crushed femur. Broken bones give scientists important clues about what happened to the animal after it died.

C N

This is a prickly pear cactus. In the summer, its red and yellow flowers can be seen in the area surrounding CLDQ.

C N

This cabin, located in the Twin Peaks area, was part of a settlement from about 1900. The cabin is over 100 years old.

Everyone Needs a Home

People and dinosaurs share some of the same needs. Every dinosaur needed a place to live. An animal's (or dinosaur's) home is called its habitat.

An animal's habitat includes food, shelter, and water.

Draw a picture of your habitat. Then draw a picture of your favorite dinosaur's habitat. In both pictures, label food, shelter, and water.

Your Habitat

Dinosaur's Habitat

Excavation of a Dinosaur Bone

Excavation techniques change with time. Paleontologists used to focus only on the bones. Surrounding sediments were ignored.

Modern paleontologists, like modern forensic scientists, know that everything around a specimen is a potential clue.

Look at the "story of a bone" panel in the visitors' center. Write the number of each step on the picture it goes with on the next page.

1. Remove overlying rock and expose the fossil.

2. Apply special glues to consolidate the fossil and to prevent loss of smaller fragments.

3. Surround the fossil with a protective "field jacket" made of burlap and plaster, and dig away the surrounding rock.

4. Transport field jacket with the fossil to the paleontological laboratory.

5. Prepare the fossil by removing surrounding rock, or "matrix," and re-attaching small bone fragments with special glues.

6. Curate in a museum where the fossil, associated clues, maps, notes, and important information may be studied and used to reassemble the puzzle.

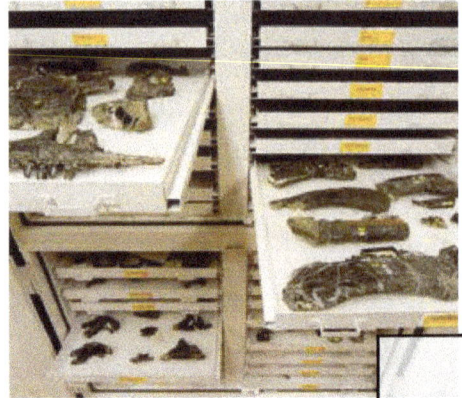

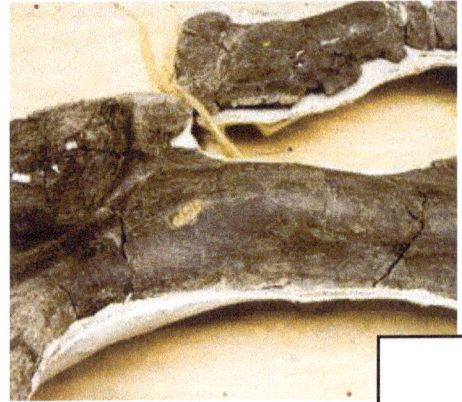

Jurassic Crossword

Clues:

Across:

2. 66% of all the bones found at Cleveland-Lloyd belong to the _____.

3. Cleveland-Lloyd Dinosaur _____.

6. Meat eater

8. Cleveland-Lloyd is the densest _____ of Jurassic age dinosaur bones.

10. What sauropod's leg is found in the visitors' center.

11. Long-necked plant eater.

Down:

1. Who donated $10,000 in 1941?

4. What age (geologic time period) are the bones found at Cleveland-Lloyd?

5. Plant eater

7. The fossils found in the quarry.

9. Preserved plant or animal remains from the distant past.

BLM Emblem

NATIONAL SYSTEM OF PUBLIC LANDS

U.S. DEPARTMENT OF THE INTERIOR
BUREAU OF LAND MANAGEMENT

This is the emblem of the Bureau of Land Management.

An emblem is a symbol designed to represent an idea or message. In the box , design your own Cleveland-Lloyd Dinosaur Quarry emblem. Your emblem should include important parts of Cleveland-Lloyd Dinosaur Quarry . Someone who has never seen CLDQ should be able to learn something about it just by looking at your emblem.

www.ingramcontent.com/pod-product-compliance
Lightning Source LLC
Chambersburg PA
CBHW081238020426
42331CB00012B/3216